A PRAYER GUIDE FOR PARENTS AND GRANDPARENTS

TRANSFORMING CHILDREN'S LIVES THROUGH PRAYER

Joy Ani

FOREWORD

A PRAYER GUIDE FOR PARENTS AND GRANDPARENTS TRANSFORMING CHILDREN'S LIVES THROUGH PRAYER

So much has been said, written and indeed achieved through the efficacy, power and art of prayer. Those of us who give ourselves even moderately to prayer are well aware of its role in determining the quality of our lives and success as well as that of our loved ones.

To think that prayer can also be a potent tool in helping to determine the physical shape, health, character, choices, relationships and emotions of our children is hugely reassuring. Scripture clearly states that Jesus grew in every area of life and especially in stature; this is a clear indication that God is concerned about how each child turns out in life. The author of this book, by the revelation of the Spirit, helps us capture a very salient part of this submission, the force behind Jesus' growth in all areas—and that is prayer.

It will amaze you to realise that nothing happened on earth in the life of Jesus that was not the product of prayer. Without a doubt, He would have been prayed for by His parents and the significant people in His life. We are told in scripture in Luke 2:37-40 that Anna had spent the larger part of her life praying in the temple for Israel and the Messiah, so it is no surprise that verse 40 tells us that *'the child grew, and waxed strong in spirit, filled with wisdom: and the grace of God was upon him'*.

The psalmist again confirmed this in Psalm 144:11-12, where he recorded this prayer: *'Rid me, and deliver me from the hand of strange children, whose mouth speaketh vanity, and their right hand is a right hand of falsehood: That our sons may be as plants grown up in their youth; that our daughters may be as corner stones, polished after the similitude of a palace.'*

Goodness, how often we have neglected to exercise this grace over our children! Indeed, our prayers can work wonders as God works in their lives—and this book brings this truth to the fore. I strongly recommend it to anyone and everyone who has the desire to see their children reach their maximum potential.

God bless the author for opening herself up to the Spirit to receive such light for our generation and generations yet to come. Please read this yourself and also recommend it to everyone you know. This book is a manual to mould a child's destiny.

Rev Mrs Lyne Oladapo
Compassionate Jesus People Ministry
Lagos, Nigeria

REVIEWS

I'll like to congratulate Joy Ani for the publication of this powerful tool that I believe every parent, guardian and grandparent should invest into.

I have come to realise over the years, that our prayers for our children are the best and most lasting legacy that can be passed on to them.

This book is packed with prayerful declarations that you can begin to speak over the lives of your children and grandchildren.

I'd like to encourage you to begin to speak to God about your child—you can start by using the powerful declarations in this book.

Thank you, Joy, for pouring your heart out and for praying for our children and grandchildren.

I pray that the Lord will reward you and cause this book to be a blessing to many.

Shola Alabi
www.sholaalabi.com

This prayer guide for parents and grandparents is what is needed at this crucial time in our history. This book is not just an eye-opener to the prevalent decadence among our youth and the best way to tackle the problems through the power of prayers, but can equally be seen as a gift to all parents in the task of bringing up morally-fit children in this present society. Our neighbourhoods are crowded with unruly children from different dysfunctional backgrounds, and this menace has contributed to not only the breakdown of law and order in the home and society, but has also impeded the majority of the children from fulfilling their destinies.

Joy has been able to deal with the different facets of our children's lives in this book, tapping into the power of prayer and providing a tool for parents and grandparents for the re-shaping and re-defining their children's lives—with the ultimate goal of helping them to fulfil their destinies. The book also tries to highlight to parents and grandparents the fundamental need to be on fire spiritually, in order to stand as a shield around their children.

Bimbo Otesanya
Author
London UK

I congratulate Reverend Joy Ani for putting together this prayer guide for parents and grandparents. Life on earth is very interesting and strategic; it can be shaped from the beginning for maximum impact, contributing to the progress of humanity, while ensuring maximum advancement in an atmosphere of peace that passes all understanding. All this is accomplished only if our parents and grandparents are able to bring us up in the wisdom of God, our days watered by prayer. With the power of Heaven working on our behalf, we cannot fail but to fulfil God's plan and purpose for our lives.

In 2 Timothy 1:5, the Apostle Paul gives a powerful account of a young man he fathered in ministry. This young man, Timothy, had a combination of both a mother and grandmother's prayers, combined with the Word, which built a strong faith in him. This enabled him to become an effective disciple—one who was beneficial to Paul's ministry, the body of Christ and society at large.

I believe that this guide for parents and grandparents is spot on to help parents and grandparents to raise their children and grandchildren up in the fear of God.

I highly recommend every parent and grandparent invest in this book—it will save you a lot of headache.

Bishop Ben Osei Owusu Ansah
Jubilee Christian Ministry International
President of Kingdom Partnership International UK

Thank you, Joy Ani, for answering the call to put this prayer guide for parents and grandparents together. This will help and guide many parents on how to pray for their children, grandchildren and great-grandchildren, as well as children in our community.

I highly recommend this book to anyone that wants to see children's lives transformed.

Reverend Nicholas Nunayon
Executive Director
Kingsgen Foundation

Nick Nunayon B.A, MSc, MTh, PTTLS, OCP.
Jesus loves you and cares for you. Give your life to Him.
www.Kingsgen.co.uk
www.kingsgenacademy.co.uk
www.biblelifechristiancentre.org

This book by Rev. Joy Ani is a must-have for every family! In this book, Joy delves deep into the core of prayer; she beautifully outlines the importance and the power of prayer and its positive impact on the next generation. I highly recommend this book to every parent and grandparent.

Vida Lartey, Parents Shield UK

First of all, I want to congratulate Pastor Mrs Joy Ani for showing gratitude to God at the birth of her grandson and allowing herself to be used by Him to write this empowering prayer guide. God will reward her indeed.

As we know from scriptures, there were several women who stood in the gap to pray for their children until they became successful. In Exodus 2:I, Jochebed, the mother of Moses, kept and prayed for Moses when all other male children were being thrown in the River Nile. I believe Jochebed's prayer kept her child in the king's palace and in the land of Midian until his return as a deliverer of the Israelites. Jochebed's prayer shaped Moses's destiny. As Pastor Joy rightly says, "It is vital that we pray…even for the unborn child".

Hannah, Elkanah's wife, also prayed for Samuel

whilst the child was in the womb. She dedicated him to God as a Nazirite, and when she presented him to Eli in 1 Samuel 1:27, she said, "For this child I prayed, and the Lord has granted me my request which I asked of him." Hannah also prayed that her son would one day become a priest unto God, so she made Samuel a linen ephod (Priestly garment) every year and brought it to Shiloh.

This prayer guide is truly a must-have in every Christian home. I highly recommend it for all those who are passionate to see orderliness in the lives of their children. I believe, as parents and grandparents continue to pray for their children, they will see God's goodness and His promises manifest in their lives, in Jesus' name.

Reverend Mrs Margaret Maccarthy
Founder and Senior Pastor of Shalom Ministries
International

DEDICATION

I dedicate this book to my amazing grandson, Prince Zane. Through his birth, God reassured me that He answers prayers. My prayer for you is that at a tender age you will give your life to the Lord and fulfil His plan and purpose for you. Your birth gave birth to this book. Grandma loves you.

To my wonderful children, both biological and spiritual. I commit you to God, Who can keep you from falling away. I will not mourn concerning any of you, in Jesus' Name.

This book is also dedicated to all parents and grandparents who want to pray and make a difference in the lives of their children, grandchildren and the young people in the land.

ACKNOWLEDGEMENTS

I am grateful to God for inspiring me to put this book together.

I am sincerely grateful to God for blessing me with parents that dedicated their lives to prayer. My parents were people with a rare passion for prayer, especially my mum, whose fervency for praying earned her the nickname of 'a praying woman'. I watched my parents pray several times a day, and they taught me to do the same. I thank them from the bottom of my heart, for what they have instilled in me has made a tremendous impact and made me who I have become today.

WITH SPECIAL THANKS

To Pastor Oyinlola Bukky Akande (OBA) for your word of wisdom, encouragement and prayer for this project to materialisation you are indeed a blessing. I love you always.

To my gifted editors, (The Editor's Chair) Denise Roberts you are terrific, thank you for your invaluable input.

To Rev Mrs Lyne Oladapo for making out time out of your busy schedules to write the foreward of this book. Heaven will surely reward you abundantly.

My special thanks goes to all the reviewers of this book, (Shola Alabi, Bimbo Otesanya, Bishop Ben Osei Owusu Ansah, Nick Nunayon, Vida Lartey and Reverend Mrs Margaret Maccarthy) out of your busy schedules you have suspended other things to read the manuscript and reviewed it, my prayer for you is that if God need to suspend any elements to answer your prayers, He will do so even as he suspended the sun to give Joshua victory. Joshua 10:12-14.

To the many authors whose their prayer books have been a blessing to me. I have read several books on the subject of prayer and some I can't even remember the title or the author's name, nonetherless, my prayer life has been impacted by those authors and I say thank you.

God gives us people along the way who help make our dreams come through. I'm especially thankful to Chindah Chindah, my publisher. Exatly a year ago I shared the vision with you and you believed in the vision and you agreed to take on the publishing of the book. Thank you for your patience with me. God's time is truly the best and He makes all things beautify in His time.

My prayer for myself and my readers is that God will help us to leave a legacy of faith/prayer as we intercessed for our children, grandchildren and unborn generations in Jesus name.

CONTENTS

INTRODUCTION

I believe in prayer and the God that answers prayers, our earnest petitions can unlock any door. Prayer is the master key to solving difficult problems and to triumph over stubborn situations. Prayer is a gift and a privilege offered to us by God. When He says, *'Come to me, come let us reason together, come as you are,'* this a call from our Heavenly Father who wants to have communion with us. How I wish we could all answer this call, especially on behalf of our children and grandchildren.

Prayer is power, and it changes things. It doesn't matter how far or for what period of time your child or your grandchild may have wandered away from God, prayer can bring him or her back. However, you might be saying that my child or grandchild does not know God. If you can pray and intercede for him or her, your prayer will do wonders before your very eyes. Trust me, your child will eventually surrender to God—if you do not relent in prayer or give up so easily.

God is waiting for you to intercede on behalf of that child. Interestingly, you don't have to be biological parents or grandparents to stand in the gap. God said in Ezekiel 22:30, *'So I sought for a man among them who would make a wall and stand in the gap before Me on behalf of the land, that I should not destroy it, but I found no one.'* Will you be that man or that woman who will stand in the gap for the children and grandchildren? Will you be that spiritual parent and grandparent for those lives wasting away because of lack of a man or a woman to pray? God is counting on you and me to say, 'Yes Lord, I want you to use me to bring healing and restoration to the children of this land.' God is constantly seeking for that person.

The Bible says in the book of Lamentations 2:19, *'Pour out your heart like water before the face of the Lord. Lift your hands toward Him for the life of your young children.'*

The number of deadly knife stabbings at the time of writing in 2019, according to Murder Map, is 67 in London alone. That amounts to over half of the total number of homicides committed in the capital so far in the same year, which currently sits at 112. And 2018 was London's bloodiest in ten years, with the total number of homicides being 132.

2

According to the news in various newspapers, London Mayor Sadiq Khan said that violent crime in the capital was being addressed 'through combining tough policing with a public health approach...' He said his office was prioritising efforts towards tackling violence and knife crime but was under great strain. The problem, according to Mr Khan, is a series of budget cuts which has resulted in the loss of billions of pounds from the Met Police budget over the last eight years.

He went on to say, 'I'm hoping that the Home Secretary today is able to satisfy the demands made by chief constables across the country, including the Met Police commissioner, we need money now and it can pay for a surge in policing, increased overtime, using money to make sure we have officers doing more work around the clock.' (www.metro.co.uk, 2019)

We can understand the call for more resources to help fight violent crime, which, as we're all aware, represents such a tiny percentage of the problems we face in society, but God has also promised to be our very present help in this time of trouble. We don't have to stand back helplessly and hold our breath while the future of society (our children) are being destroyed. We can make a difference through prayer. Hence, the birth of this book as a wake-up call to parents, grandparents and intercessors to rise up and call upon the Lord who is worthy to be praised, so that we can be saved from our enemies.

NOTES/REFLECTION ON INTRODUCTION

Lamentations 2:19, *'Pour out your heart like water before the face of the Lord. Lift your hands toward Him for the life of your young children*

What is that one issue you want God to solve for your child or grandchild right now? Note it down as a prayer request with the date and talk to God about it. When it has been answered, come back to note the testimony and the date.

The reason for this exercise is to ask, receive and thank God for it—and to build your faith that prayer works.

PRAYER OF SALVATION

Do you know God for yourself? Before you can be an effective intercessor for your children and grandchildren, you have to know whom you believe. You cannot pray to an unknown God effectively, therefore, it's mandatory to be born again. You need to cultivate a close relationship with your Heavenly Father before you can pray for your children and grandchildren to also know the Lord.

Please pray this short prayer with all your heart and believe it, because the Bible says in the book of John 3:16, *'For God loved the world so much that he gave his only Son. God gave his Son so that whosoever believes in him may not be lost but have eternal life.'*

Prayer: Dear Jesus, I know I am a sinner and I can't save myself. I believe You died on the cross to pay for my sins. Please come into my heart and forgive my sins. I give You my life from now on, be my Saviour and my Master in Jesus' Name. Amen.

Congratulations! You are now born again, and you can have the assurance that God hears you and answers your prayer.

NOTES/REFLECTION ON SALVATION PRAYER

Have you given your life to Jesus? If yes, note the date down to as close as you can remember.

Are you making progress in your walk with the Lord? If not, why? You will need to read your Bible and pray regularly to make progress in your walk with the Lord.

Did you give your life to Jesus as a result of picking up this book? Note down how you feel about your salvation.

CHAPTER 1

CHILDREN'S SPIRITUAL WELL-BEING

Each stage of your child or your grandchild's life comes with so much emotion. I still remember the sight of my first child although it was over 27 years ago. It seems just like yesterday; the joy of holding her in my arms was so enormous that, at one point, I couldn't believe she was my daughter. The only thing that comes to mind is just adoration to the Lord, thanking Him for His marvellous gifts. I have watched her grow from one stage of life to another; from playgroup to university, getting her first job and getting married.

My joy also knew no bounds when I held my first grandchild in my arms and, again, I thanked Jesus for another blessing. Why am I saying this? Just to let you know that children are a heritage from the Lord, and it is a huge privilege to be a parent or grandparent. Therefore, it is wise to commit our children and grandchildren back to the Lord every day. We are just custodians, and we shall give an account to God about how well we handled that which He committed into our hands. Considering this, it is paramount to stand in the gap for all our children and grandchildren.

Whether it's your first child or your last, or your first grandchild, you would do well to pray for every area of their lives.

PRAY FOR YOUR CHILDREN AND GRANDCHILDREN'S SPIRITUAL LIVES

It is vital that we pray for them—even the unborn child or grandchild's salvation—as they have to make vital decisions for their lives at one point or the other. This is a personal decision that we cannot make for them and so we owe them our prayers—that the eyes of their understanding may be opened and that they would make this decision at a very early stage of their lives. I cannot overemphasise how crucial it is that we pray for their relationship with God and their spiritual well-being—because the spiritual realm controls the physical. If any child is lacking in a good relationship with God, you can be sure that, sooner or later, it will affect every other area of his/her life.

We should pray for the salvation of any unsaved child and thank God for the salvation of those who are saved.

For God so loved the world that He gave His only begotten Son, that whoever believes in Him should not perish but have everlasting life. John 3:16 NKJV.

PRAYER POINTS FOR THE SPIRITUAL LIVES OF OUR CHILDREN AND GRANDCHILDREN

God in heaven, to You all flesh shall come, I pray for the salvation of my children and grandchildren, that at a tender age they will come to know You and give their lives to You, in Jesus' Name.

Father God, I pray that my children and grandchildren will be saved, no-one comes to You except You draw him or her to Yourself. Father, I pray that my children and grandchildren will not escape Your reach, that when You call, they will hear You and that when You draw them to Yourself, they will not resist Your pulling and nudging, in Jesus' Name.

I pray, Lord, that my children and grandchildren will

know You as the only true God, and Jesus Christ, their Saviour, whom You have sent to save them, in Jesus' Name.

Father God, I ask that my children and grandchildren love You with all their hearts with all their souls, with all their strength, and with all their mind and that their hearts will pant after you, O God. That their souls will thirst for God; You, only the living God, that they will not go after other gods.

Father God, I pray that my children and grandchildren will always come to You for help, that no matter the situation, that they will hope in You, the God of their salvation.

Lord, I pray that my children and grandchildren will never run away from You, even when they make a mistake by way of error or sin, that they will always come to You in repentance. And as they do so, Lord, may they receive Your forgiveness, even as You have promised, in Jesus' Name.

Father God, I am confident of this—that You have begun a good work in the lives of my children and grandchildren and that You will bring to completion that which You have started, that my children and grandchildren will not backslide, they will not deny

You, no matter the situation, that You will be with them till the end of the world—even as You have promised, in Jesus' Name.

Lord Jesus, I pray that my children and grandchildren will forever remain in You as You remain in them; that they will know that outside of You they cannot bear any good fruit. Let them know that they are a branch in You and they cannot succeed without attaching permanently to the vine, which is You, Lord. Help them to be firmly grounded and rooted in You—this I pray, in Jesus' Name.

Father God, I pray that You will lead my children and grandchildren to a genuine Bible-believing church where they can be stirred up in love to do good works and they will enjoy fellowship with other believers. As they do Lord, I pray that the gifts in them will be identified, nurtured and developed to serve the body of Christ in Jesus' Name.

Father God, I pray for my children and grandchildren that they will love Your Word so much that they will not be able to live without it; that it will be a delight unto them and honey to their taste. I pray that my children and grandchildren will study Your Word, meditate on it and that they will live out Your Word all the days of their lives, in Jesus' Name.

Father, I know Your Name and I trust in You to help me raise my children and grandchildren in Your way. I know that as I seek You, You will not forsake me nor my children or grandchildren, to the fourth generation. I pray that, even if Jesus tarries, my lineage will never depart from knowing You as their Lord and Saviour.

Above all, Father, as my children and grandchildren know You and serve You, may they be true disciples to all nations and make You known to others, and disciple others as well. I thank You because You have promised to be with them always, even to the end of the age, in Jesus' Name. Amen.

NOTES/REFLECTION ON CHILDREN'S SALVATION AND SPIRITUAL WELL-BEING

Is your child or grandchild born again? If not, pray about it. If he or she is, then note here how you feel about his or her walk with the Lord. It may give you some ideas on how to pray.

What about his or her prayer life? Perhaps this is something you can pray about right now.

CHAPTER 2

CHILDREN'S PHYSICAL WELLNESS

We take care of our physical bodies by following a balanced diet and exercising, but unfortunately, even after all sorts of exercise and special diets, many young people today do not love themselves or like the way they look. Of course, this is not a problem that affects young people alone. There are men and women of all ages who are seriously not content with their physical bodies. They can not accept who they are; many go through all sorts of painful surgery to change their look or their sex; to make themselves become what they are not, and this is heartbreaking. Some have also developed eating disorders, such as anorexia and bulimia nervosa, due to distorted images of themselves. We would do well to stand against such a spirit.

It is even more heartbreaking when young people fall prey to this spirit. Their bodies are still developing and long-term eating disorders can lead to further problems such as infertility, poor blood circulation, osteoporosis and heart failure. They can also experience psychological problems such as depression, anxiety and paranoia. It can be devastating for parents and grandparents to watch their children go through such anguish. Nothing you tell them can convince them there is nothing wrong with their bodies or the way they look. Therefore, I cannot overemphasise the importance of parents and grandparents' roles in standing in the gap in this area—your prayers can spare them from this kind of misery. Some of the children's problems are more than just the desire to look good... it could be a spiritual battle as well. You need the guidance of the Holy Spirit to be able to discern how and what to pray about.

PRAYER POINTS FOR THE PHYSICAL NEEDS OF YOUR CHILDREN AND GRANDCHILDREN

Father God, I declare and decree according to Your Word that my children and grandchildren are fearfully and wonderfully made, for Your works concerning them are marvellous; there is nothing missing, nothing broken in their lives.

Father God, I pray for my children and grandchildren that they will keep their hearts with all diligence, for out of it flow the issues of life. Lord, let my children and grandchildren not fall into sexual immorality; let them know the implication of it—and, as a result, flee from it. Holy Spirit, help them to remember that their body is Your temple and they are not the owner of their bodies because Jesus Christ has paid the price for them. As a result of that, may they always glorify God in their bodies and in their spirits, which belong to God.

Father God, by the authority You have given me, I stand against any eating disorders in my children and grandchildren's lives, and I say no to anorexia, bulimia or to any kinds of bad eating habits.

Father God, I pray that my children and grandchildren will not defile the temple of God, which is their body, for the temple of God must be holy.

Father God, I stand in the gap for my children and grandchildren. I ask, by Your mercies, that You will help them to present their bodies as a living sacrifice, holy, acceptable to You, which is their reasonable service.

Father God, I pray that my children would not buy into the lies of the devil on how they should look; that they would not be influenced by the lure of fashion magazines, television, or movies which present to them a wrong identity, but they would know that true identity is from You, and thereby, would put on the Lord Jesus Christ and make no provision for the flesh, to fulfil its lusts.

Father God, I pray that when my children and grandchildren are weak You supply them with your strength. Let their flesh not control them and let sin not have dominion over them, for they are more than conquerors and able to do all things through Your power.

NOTES/REFLECTION ON CHILDREN'S PHYSICAL WELL-BEING

Do you take note of your child or grandchild's appearance?

Does he or she eat well?

Romans 12:1-2 (NKJV)
I beseech you therefore, brethren, by the mercies of God, that you present your bodies a living sacrifice, holy, acceptable to God, *which is* your reasonable service. And do not be conformed to this world, but be transformed by the renewing of your mind, that you may prove what *is* that good and acceptable and perfect will of God.

CHAPTER 3

CHILDREN'S INTERPERSONAL RELATIONSHIPS

Praying for our children and grandchildren's relationships can never be overemphasised. If you look back over your life to when you were a child, you will remember that when you had friction with your parents or grandparents, most of the time, it was because you lacked understanding of the fact that as loving parents, they wanted to do all they could to protect you. We sometimes think they are depriving us of our rights and privileges, or infringing on our privacy. Unfortunately, sometimes relationships with children and grandchildren break down but before this happens—and during that period—you can pray.

In other words, praying for a good relationship with our children and grandchildren is vital. They should be able to run back to us when issues of life beat them down. It's sad when a parent has to bear the guilt of a child committing suicide—even though it might not be their fault. Parents will always feel that they could have done more to prevent mishaps or unfortunate situations but, in most cases, they have done all they can. At such a time when all you have left is prayer, it's important to know that your children and grandchildren belong to God. You must, therefore, allow Him to work in you the grace to commit them into His hands so that He can change the situation.

Praying for our children and grandchildren's relationships with their siblings is equally important, as we will not be here forever. There is comfort in knowing that their relationships are good and that they relate well to and value one another. In the book of Psalms 133:1-3, the writer exclaims, 'how good and pleasant it is for brothers (and sisters) to live together in unity …' and closes off by saying, 'for there the Lord commanded the blessing, even life forevermore'. When our relationships are good they bring health and life to us; when they are bad they can drain us of the very same. You see, as parents and grandparents, our roles and responsibilities in this aspect of our children and grandchildren's lives are crucial. Many of us have witnessed strife between siblings in our lifetime, with family members not talking to one another and even murdering one another through envy, jealousy or bitterness. It's distressing for parents and grandparents to witness such disharmony! We want to know that our children and grandchildren will continue to relate to one another in harmony when we are no longer here to witness it.

You must have read or heard the story of Abel and Cain in the Bible. Adam and Eve gave birth to two sons, Cain and Abel. Cain, a farmer, offers God a portion of his crops one day as a sacrifice, only to learn that God is more pleased with Abel's fattest portion of his flocks... In anger, Cain kills his brother. Please read the whole of the story in the Bible; Genesis chapter 4.

A similar story of siblings planning evil against one another can be seen in the Biblical story of Joseph, sold into slavery by his brothers who were jealous of his dream and being his father's favourite. He was assigned as a slave in Potiphar's household. Please read the whole of the story in Genesis chapter 37 to 50 as there are important lessons that we can learn from the passage as parents and grandparents. We do not want to end up grieving over our children as a result of us not taking our place in prayer.

I remember when my baby sister and I experienced a major breach in our relationship—it took years for the issues to be resolved as our parents were no longer alive to intervene. However, throughout that period, I kept the door of my heart and the door of my home open, waiting for the time when my sister would return. I also wished my little sister good, believing that a day would come when she would realise how much I loved her and repent of her actions.

Truly, God sees my heart! He answered the prayer through a genuine man of God that noticed the state of our relationship and took it upon himself to help resolve the issues between us. God is still in the business of using people who hear His voice to help where needed. If your children's relationship with you or any members of your family is currently sour, keep praying, keep believing and God will surely intervene. Do not leave it to chance, because prayer does change things. It's sad to see families split apart, individual members having nothing to do with one another, even in their old age. Be a peacemaker as a parent and grandparent; do everything within your power to pursue the things which make for peace in your children and grandchildren's lives.

PRAYER POINTS FOR OUR CHILDREN'S AND GRANDCHILDREN'S RELATIONSHIPS

Father, in the Name of Jesus, if there are any unresolved misunderstandings between my children and grandchildren, I pray that, by Your Spirit, You will touch their hearts and that You will drive out the wedge of division and bring healing. I pray that, henceforth, there will be peace and no strain, breach, misunderstanding, argument, fight, or separation of ties between them. I pray for a forgiving heart for them, in Jesus' Name.

Father, I pray that You would instil love and compassion in them for all family members—love that is strong and unending like a cord that cannot be broken. I pray that my children and grandchildren will act in godly humility toward one another, being patient and loving with each other. Help them to make every effort to strengthen the bond of peace in our family, in Jesus' mighty Name.

Father, I pray in the Name of Jesus, as You instructed us in Your Word, that we should be of one mind and have compassion for one another; loving one another as brothers and sisters, tender-hearted and courteous. Help my children and grandchildren to obey Your

Word and do accordingly, in Jesus' Name.

Father, I pray that You would help and empower my children and grandchildren to put away all falsehood and that they would always tell the truth, even when it seems difficult to do so. I pray that they will know the joy and peace of being a truthful person. Father, as they tell the truth, may You stand by them to encourage them that it's the right thing to do—even if they get into trouble for saying and doing what is right in Your sight, in Jesus' Name.

Father, I pray that my children and grandchildren would not be fools by remaining angry for longer than necessary. Your Word says that anger rests in the bosom of a fool. Help them to be quick to forgive, in Jesus' Name.

NOTES/REFLECTION ON CHILDREN'S INTERPERSONAL RELATIONSHIPS

How is your relationship with your child and grandchild, do you relate well?

What about his/her relationship with other members of the family, such as siblings, aunts, uncles and cousins?

CHAPTER 4

CHILDREN'S EDUCATIONAL AND CAREER PROGRESS

My experience as a parent is probably like most other parents, in the sense that when your baby is young, you are waiting eagerly for them to grow up, so that you can enrol them in the nursery—or at least to start attending a playgroup. The first day of leaving your child behind in the nursery probably was the best and the worst day of your life, as you turned your back, still hearing your child crying. This made you feel like you were making a wrong decision letting go of your child and entrusting them into the hands of another person. I would encourage every parent to start praying about their children's future education—even before they conceive—that God would make every stage of their education easy and smooth.

Little did I realise that I would have to confront a big challenge in acquiring a place for my child at the nursery school. I had to go through several appeals to secure a place for her and, from there on, the battle continued even until the time of getting her a preferred secondary school. That time, I had to appeal seven times before she got into the school. I have since become wiser and know I needed to battle it out in the spirit also. Why, am I telling you this? I want you to realise that we need to pray for every area of our children's lives well in advance of the 'need' to pray. As a grandparent now, I am joining my faith in praying for my grandchild that everything about his life shall flow smoothly.

Not only do we have to pray for them to get into school, but we also need to pray for our children and grandchildren to develop the ability and desire to learn—we cannot take it for granted! Even when a child is still in the womb, we can pray that everything about the child will be knitted together with a good, strong, healthy mind and body, and they would be taught by God. The earlier we start praying for our children and grandchildren, the better for us and them. However, prayer does not know age barriers; no matter the age of our children and grandchildren, they can still benefit from your prayer for their academic success.

You also need to be specific in praying for your children's career choice. Pray that it will be what God has purposed for them for their destiny, and that they would not choose their career based on what their parents or grandparents want them to do, what their friends are doing, or what is selling at that moment. Some children have entered into the entertainment world, just because it is popular and because there is more money and fame from such professions. Some of them want to be footballers because they have seen sportsmen making money and gaining popularity. Unfortunately, most parents make the mistake of wanting their children to study certain courses or go into a profession because they believe their children would make more money and acquire fame from it. Hence, many of the children end up studying what they do not enjoy, and they end up getting degree after degree and still not making progress in their careers. I therefore encourage parents and grandparents to pay serious attention to the choice of career their children and grandchildren venture into, as this can go a long way to determine whether they will fulfil their God-ordained destiny.

PRAYER POINTS FOR OUR CHILDREN'S AND GRANDCHILDREN'S EDUCATION AND CAREERS

Father, in the Name of Jesus I pray. You have promised in Your Word that all our children (including our grandchildren) shall be taught of the Lord, and great shall be their peace. Father, may the peace of God be my children and grandchildren's portion regarding their studies, right from early years until their last breath, in Jesus' Name.

Father, give my children and grandchildren a good mind, teachable spirit, and the ability to learn. Instil in them the desire to attain knowledge and skill, and may they have joy in the process of learning, in Jesus' Name.

Father, according to Your Word, I ask that my children and grandchildren will apply their heart to instruction, and their ears to words of knowledge and I pray that You, Lord, will give them understanding in all things, in Jesus' Name.

Heavenly Father, I ask You to put a consuming desire for wisdom in my children and grandchildren; a consuming desire for wisdom in their academic studies. Lord, as they set their mind to learn, let

knowing You and Your Word also be their priority—
and as they do this, may they reap a hundred-fold
reward in their studies; may they enjoy the fruits of
their labour, in Jesus' Name.

Father, I pray that my children and grandchildren will
not depend on their own understanding when it
comes to making the very important decision of
choosing the right subjects for the best career path for
them to follow, in Jesus' Name. I praise You, Lord, for
I have confidence that You will direct their path as
they lean on You.

Father, thank You, because Your plans and purposes
for my children and grandchildren's lives are good
and not evil; plans to prosper and not to harm them
and to give them a hope and a future. Reveal the
plans You have for my children and grandchildren, in
Jesus' Name.

Father, in the Name of Jesus, I ask that You anoint my
children and grandchildren with the spirit of
excellence, intelligence, divine vision, knowledge and
understanding for accelerated progress in every area
of their lives.

Father, in the Name of Jesus, I prophesy into the lives
of my children and grandchildren, that their lives

shall be wonderful and that their lives shall shine and they shall be favoured above their mates and they shall stand out for good all the days of their lives.

Father, let Your power upgrade the brains of my children and my grandchildren for excellent performance in their academic pursuits, in the Name of Jesus.

O God my Father, position my children for uncommon success and make their lives a wonder and a testimony, in the Name of Jesus.

My father and my God, equip my children and grandchildren with wisdom, knowledge and understanding to be successful in all areas of their lives, and let their lives advertise Your glory, in the Name of Jesus.

Father, in the Name of Jesus, let my children be promoted in every area of their lives because they have the mind of Christ.

Father, let my children and grandchildren work with all of their hearts in their studies and career because they recognise that they are working for You and not men.

Father, bless the studies and careers of my children and my grandchildren. May they see the fruit of their studies and let Your favour rest upon them and establish the work of their hands for them.

My Father and my God, let my children and grandchildren experience academic excellence in their studies and in their careers, in the mighty Name of Jesus.

Father, promotion comes from You and not from any man, because You are the One that can raise up one and unseat the other. I ask that You would promote my children and grandchildren in their academic arenas, jobs and businesses, sit them among the rulers in society, and let them be relevant and sought after in the decision-making of the land, in Jesus' Name.

NOTES/REFLECTION ON CHILDREN'S EDUCATION AND CAREER PROGRESS

Do you check your child or grandchild's actual and predicted grades?

Is he or she working towards it or behind? Do you need to seek support?

Have you had conversations about his/her career aspirations?

CHAPTER 5

CHILDREN'S FINANCIAL AWARENESS

If we are to look at finance from the right perspective, then I think we must begin by asking, what is money and why do we need to teach our children and grandchildren about it?

Modern society defines money as a tool by which we get to buy what we want. While society also recognises that money enhances a person's living conditions I think we often underestimate its importance to almost every area of our lives. In real life, money influences almost every choice we make... money helps people achieve a better quality of education, a greater chance of business success and higher work output.

From the above definition, you can see that money is an essential commodity that helps us run our lives. Even though people say money cannot buy everything, thinking practically, money is the basic thing that is used to determine a person's social status. If money is so important, and it can also lead to freedom or slavery, parents and grandparents would be wise to educate their children about it.

Money, wealth and possessions are so important that the Bible talks about it more than 2300 times. According to Wealthwithpurpose.com, Jesus spoke about money in roughly 15 per cent of his preaching and 11 out of 39 parables.

God expects us to teach our children about money because the Bible says we cannot serve two masters—either we will serve God or money. Since this book is not a finance management book, I will not go into details, but please read the book of Matthew 6: 19-24. It is also not enough to just teach your children, you also need to demonstrate to your children and grandchildren a better way of handling money—which means you also need to educate yourself if you are not savvy in this area. Still, the first step is to pray for your children and grandchildren's finances, and this chapter will give you a starting point for how to do it.

It is important to know that it is never too early to begin teaching your children and grandchildren about money. As soon as they learn to use money, they can learn the fundamental principles about managing it. How blessed they are if they have parents and grandparents who love them and also teach them how to manage their money. The training which children receive from their parents will stick with them throughout their lives.

This can be the basis on which their financial success stands. I also want you to know that your children and grandchildren still have a personal responsibility to practise what you teach them. Therefore, do not be discouraged if they decide to have a different perspective or lifestyle about money, one that's completely different from what you taught them.

I am fortunate to have had savvy parents in the area of money management. They believed that you should multiply the money that comes into your hands, that a borrower is a slave to the lender and, therefore, I was taught I should never borrow if I do not want to be a slave to anyone. My parents also taught me that the hand of the giver is always on top and I should learn to be a giver. This teaching was so much engraved in me, even though it was only years later, when I came to England and gave my life to Christ, that I realised that all that my parents were teaching me were Bible principles.

With this teaching from my parents, my life has been so enriched because I do not find myself in the bondage of borrowing. Today, when I think about it from the perspective of an adult and how these lessons have influenced my decisions in life, I am grateful to my parents for such a wonderful teaching.

My encouragement is that you manage your borrowing, both from individuals or a financial institution, but I am mindful that this is a prayer book and not a financial manual.

The act of giving taught by my parents whilst I was growing up has also made it possible and easy for me to comply with the principle of giving 10 per cent of my income as a tithe to my church. I am comfortable with doing it because I was taught by my parents, and I also witnessed them giving their crops and money to the mosque joyfully without complaint. I have also witnessed the blessing of God upon their lives even though they were Muslim. They might not be counted as rich or wealthy, but they were successful as they lived within their means.

You may ask, why all these stories about your parents? It is important to point out to you that your children are watching and learning from you, either by your actions or speech. May I ask you as parents and grandparents, what are you teaching your children and grandchildren? What are they learning from you about how you handle your finances?

PRAYER POINTS FOR OUR CHILDREN'S AND GRANDCHILDREN'S FINANCES

Lord, thank You that every good and perfect gift comes from You to my children and grandchildren. You are my children and grandchildren's Provider and, therefore, I am confident that they lack no good thing. Thank you, Lord, for supplying all of their needs according to Your riches in glory and for making them prosperous in every way, so they can have a surplus with which to be generous on every occasion.

Father, shield my children and grandchildren from fraudsters and dubious people. Let them not be unequally yoked with wicked people in their career and academic lives, in Jesus' Name.

My Father and my God, I terminate every spirit of stagnancy in the lives of my children and grandchildren and command them to move forward by the power of the Holy Ghost.

Father God, my children and grandchildren shall not borrow but lend to many nations because they are the head and not the tail. Father God, I pray that You will open to my children and grandchildren Your good treasure and give them rain in its season and bless the work of their hands. Lord God, empower my children and grandchildren to make wealth, for they shall remember that it is You that gives them the power to prosper.

Father, I pray that my children and grandchildren will be good stewards of all that You give them and that they will not waste resources—rather, they will learn to multiply what comes into their hands, in Jesus' Name.

NOTES/REFLECTION ON CHILDREN'S FINANCIAL AWARENESS

How good is your child or grandchild with money?

Do they have good financial awareness?

What are their spending habits like and do they regularly save?

CHAPTER 6

CHILDREN'S SOCIAL AND EMOTIONAL MINDFULNESS

Friendship is important in the lives of anyone—especially children. Therefore, it is important that, as parents and grandparents, you pray for their friendships. The best way to influence them is to pray that they would attract godly friends and role models.

As a parent or grandparent, if you reflect back to when you were young, the influence each of your friends had on you was negative, positive or neutral. My guess is that your parents would not have wanted you to keep company with some of those friends if they knew what they really got up to. Today, children's friendships are even more important. The world is changing and children are even killing other children that are supposed to be their friends. I was listening to the news about a 17-year-old girl who was stabbed several times in her own home by her boyfriend—and he made it look like the girl killed herself. This is how wicked the world has become; this boy was treated well and accepted by the family as their daughter's boyfriend, and the same boy brought the family a lifetime of pain and sorrow. This tragedy ought not to be so, therefore, if you are reading this book as a parent or grandparent and you are yet to give your life to Jesus Christ, I encourage you to do so by going to the chapter on salvation in this book. Pray the salvation prayer with all of your heart and begin a new life in Christ Jesus. Then you can intercede for your children and grandchildren, believing that God will protect them and they will make godly friends.

The story of David and Jonathan in 1 Samuel 18:1-5 is such a beautiful story of godly friendship. You must pray that God will give your children and grandchildren friends who have strong faith in God— that together they will seek and love God. The Bible asks, *'Can two walk together unless they agree?'* (Amos 3:3) precisely because God knows that there will be difficulties where two people are walking in different directions from each other. You want to see that your children and grandchildren are not being influenced to join gangs, or using or selling drugs. It is important that your children and grandchildren choose their friends carefully because the way of the wicked leads one astray. You do not want to sit down and be watching helplessly whilst your children and grandchildren are being led astray. You are not helpless.

You have the power of God and the truth of His Word. So, arise and pray in the Name of Jesus. There is a saying, 'show me your friends and I will tell you who you are'. Who are your children and grandchildren's friends? Who are their role models and who is mentoring them? You also need to pray that your children will not be unequally yoked together with unbelievers, whether in friendships, marriage or the business world. This does not mean that they do not have anything to do with unbelievers, but that they should be vigilant and careful in choosing friendships and not be too trusting with closest friends, to the point where they will be led astray.

We also need to keep a close eye on our children and grandchildren regarding who they keep company with; anyone who is sexually immoral, or covetous, or anyone who is not willing to walk in the Spirit of God or anyone whose lifestyle promotes works of the flesh is not a suitable companion for your child.

PRAYER POINTS FOR GODLY FRIENDS FOR OUR CHILDREN AND GRANDCHILDREN

Father God, I pray in the Name of Jesus that You will give my children and grandchildren godly friends that would influence them positively, also give them friends that are faithful.

I pray that my children and grandchildren will be loyal to their friends and their friends will be loyal to them, even as Jonathan and David were loyal to each other, in Jesus' Name.

Father God, I pray that my children will not be companions of fools and be destroyed. Father, help them to walk with wise friends. If they are already walking with fools, I pray that You separate them so that they will not suffer the destructions preserved for the fool. Save them from evil and ungodly friends.

Father, take away anything that would make them seek out less godly friends; direct their footsteps otherwise. Father, wherever they feel lonely, rejected or suffer low self-esteem, I pray that You will give them the assurance of who they are in Christ Jesus — that they would know that Christ is their number one Friend.

Father, do not let our children and grandchildren make friends with angry and furious men so that they would not learn their ways and set a snare for their souls.

Father God, I pray that my children and grandchildren will find a godly wife or husband at the appropriate time. As You have said: no one shall lack their mate; Father, let my children and grandchildren marry their friends and not their enemies. Father, in their finding let them obtain favour from You.

EMOTION—SOUL/MIND/HEART

The Bible says in Deuteronomy chapter 6:4-5, *'Hear, O Israel: The LORD our God, the LORD is one! You shall love the LORD your God with all your heart, with all your soul, and with all your strength.'* I strongly believe this is the sole purpose of our existence and every other thing centres around it. I also believe that the Lord is saying the same thing to parents and grandparents and He wants us to teach our children and grandchildren this commandment. It should occupy our hearts day in, day out. To sum it up, it should be in our school curriculum, Sunday school and our family meetings. Why? Because in the absence of this knowledge, all other things will fall apart.

Unfortunately, society is experiencing the consequences of not loving and acknowledging God in their daily activities. Many homes and families are falling apart. Parents are too busy to teach their children the Word of God; children are being left to social media to teach them. We see children carrying out attacks and violence because of what they have fed their hearts. They display outbursts of anger, unnecessary arguments, fights; doing things that they will later regret. Parents, grandparents and teachers, I beg of you, teach the children the Word of God as that is what will save their souls.

This leads me to my next point: what is the soul? The Bible says, in Genesis 2:7 *'And the* LORD *God formed man of the dust of the ground and breathed into his nostrils the breath of life, and man became a living being.'* You see from this verse that the word 'soul' means life. The soul is the essence of a human being. It is very important what we feed the soul with because it is what will manifest into our feelings, thoughts and, eventually, actions. Our spirit connects with God; if we do not teach our children to feed their soul with the Word of God, then their spirit cannot connect with God, and then they are left to their own devices by trying to feed their souls with addiction to gadgets, drugs, alcohol and all sorts. Their souls are longing to be filled, but, unfortunately, nothing can fill our souls apart from the Word of God. The Spirit of God brings understanding and then it's easy to surrender to God; that's when people can truly love the Lord their God with all their souls.

PRAYER POINTS FOR THE HEARTS, SOULS AND MINDS OF YOUR CHILDREN AND GRANDCHILDREN

Father God, I pray that my children and grandchildren will love You with all of their hearts, souls and might, in the mighty Name of Jesus.

Father God, I pray that my children and grandchildren would learn Your Word and hide it in their hearts so that they would not sin against You, because out of the abundance of heart, their mouths will speak. Let the word of their mouths and the meditation of their hearts be acceptable to You, oh Lord, my God.

Father, I need your help; Your Word says that I should be anxious for nothing, but in everything by prayer and supplication, with thanksgiving, I should let my requests be made known to You. Father, I am asking for the grace to do exactly that, that I will not worry over my children and grandchildren's safety, but I will pray and trust You to protect them from all evil. I rest in Your unfailing Word and I receive Your peace in Jesus' Name.

NOTES/REFLECTION ON CHILDREN'S SOCIAL AND EMOTIONAL MINDFULNESS

What can you say about your children's social and emotional mindfulness?

CHAPTER 7

CHILDREN—SCRIPTURAL DECLARATIONS

The Bible says in the book of Job 22:28, *'You shall declare a thing, and it will be established for you; so, light will shine on your ways.'*

This is comforting and encouraging to know—that whatever we say or decree or declare over our children and grandchildren shall come to pass. The power is in your mouth.

Most of the following Bible references have been turned to declarations to help you declare God's Word over the lives of your children and grandchildren. Declare them frequently and personalise them by using their own names instead of he/she.

Father God, I declare and decree that my children and grandchildren will not lack intercessors; my children shall not be destroyed because You have raised intercessors to stand in the gap for them.

My Father and my God, I declare and decree that my children and grandchildren shall know You as their only true God and the Lord Jesus Christ as their Saviour.

Father God, I declare and I decree that my children and my grandchildren shall love the Lord their God with all of their hearts, souls, strength and minds, and their neighbour as themselves.

Father, I declare and decree that my children and grandchildren's souls shall pant after God, even as the deer pants for water brooks.

Father, I declare and decree that Your plans to prosper and not to harm my children and grandchildren shall be established, and their futures shall be guaranteed according to Your Word.

Father, in the Name of Jesus, I declare and decree that great shall be the peace of my children and grandchildren as You teach them about Yourself. Thank You, Lord, that my children shall have more understanding than their teachers, for Your testimonies are their meditation.

Father God, I declare and decree that my children and grandchildren will be cheerful and not suffer heartache or crushes in the spirit.

Father God, I declare and decree that whatever my children and grandchildren's hands find to do, they shall do it with all their might, as unto the Lord.

Father God, I declare and decree that my children and grandchildren will walk with wise people and be wise themselves. They shall not be destroyed because they are not a companion of fools.

Father God, I declare and decree that my children and grandchildren shall not conform to this world, but they shall be transformed as they continue to renew their minds and do that which is acceptable to God.

Father God, I declare and decree that my children and grandchildren shall not depart from Your way at any point in their lives. If they do, I declare Your mercy will locate and draw them back.

Father God, I declare and decree that my children and grandchildren have the rule over their spirit, and they shall not be broken down like a city without walls.

Father God, I declare and decree Your favour will rest upon my children and grandchildren's lives, their education, careers and businesses and all they lay their hands upon.

Father God, I declare and decree that my children and grandchildren shall exhibit the fruit of the Spirit (love, joy, peace, forbearance, kindness, goodness, faithfulness, gentleness and self-control) in their daily walk and they shall be morally sound, bringing glory to God in all their dealings.

Father God, I declare and decree that my children and grandchildren shall lend to many nations and they shall not borrow, they shall be leaders, not servants.

NOTES/REFLECTION ON CHILDREN'S SCRIPTURAL DELARATIONS

Are you consistent in your declarations?

Have you taught your children and grandchildren how to choose and declare scripture over their own lives?

A WORD OF EXHORTATION TO PARENTS AND GRANDPARENTS

PRAYING FOR YOUR CHILDREN IS A MUST FOR EVERY LOVING PARENT/GRANDPARENT

We all want the best for our children and grandchildren so it is natural for us to be concerned when we see them walking in ways that can cause them harm. Raising children is a huge responsibility and even when they are grown they will expect you to be there for their own children too. You need to pray to God to help you because you can't do it alone. You must partner with Him, the One who has given you the responsibility to bring them up in His way. It's mandatory, as there are no perfect parents or perfect children or grandchildren. Only God is perfect and that is why it's important to seek God's face and ask for His help in parenting your children and grandchildren.

Never underestimate the power of prayer because it goes a long way to make a difference in their lives. I can testify to the power of a parent's prayer in my own life; whatever I am today, it was my parents' prayers and nurturing that made me. Even when I became an adult with my own children, my parents were still praying for me—right until the time they passed on. I miss my parents' prayers. However, the seeds of prayer they have sown are now bringing forth fruit.

Father God, I pray that You help me to learn Your Word and teach them to my children and grandchildren; help me to live by example. I pray that Your Word will be in my mouth at all times, that I will live Your Word, and as I do so, may my actions also speak to my children and grandchildren, in Jesus' Name.

Father, I need Your help. Your Word says that I should be anxious for nothing, but in everything by prayer and supplication with thanksgiving, I should let my requests be made known to You. Father, I am asking for the grace to do exactly that, that I will not worry over my children and grandchildren's safety, but I will pray and trust You to protect them from all evil. I rest in Your unfailing Word and I receive Your peace in Jesus' Name.

51 QUESTIONS TO ASK YOUR CHILD OR GRANDCHILD SO YOU KNOW WHAT TO PRAY FOR

This is a guide to questions that you might ask your child or your grandchild to give you an insight into what to pray about for him or her.

Adapt the questions to suit your child's age and level of maturity. Please use wisdom when asking questions. Create an environment of love and care before you begin.

Your motive is to see and know where your child is in their journey of life, how you can support them and, most importantly, how to pray for them.

The questions will help you to remain alert and to tackle any underlying problems before they get out of hand.

Please do not try to catch your child out, as a child can sense your motive and this can lead them to shut down or to refuse to open up at all.

I pray for wisdom and understanding for you in raising godly and resilient children, in Jesus' Name.

May God give you listening ears and eyes that see potential problems before they arise; may He ever provide you with adequate solutions.

QUESTIONS

1. How would you describe my parenting style?
2. Who would you say is your best friend right now and why?
3. What skills would you like to learn?
4. Is bullying a problem at your school?
5. What are the things that I do that annoy you?
6. What do you think about life in general?
7. Do you believe in God?
8. What do you think about God?
9. What motivates you to do what you do, e.g study/work?
10. Are there any parts of your body that you like or dislike?

11. What is a feature about yourself that you either like or dislike?

12. Do you ever feel jealous about the family of your friends, and if yes, why?

13. What are the best and worst things about having a smartphone?

14. Do you think you want to get married one day and have children of your own?

15. Are you looking forward to becoming an adult?

16. Do I praise you too much or not enough?

17. What is the one thing that I don't understand about you?

18. What would you do with a million pounds or dollars?

19. If I could buy you just one thing, what would you want that thing to be?

20. Are you happy with your friends? Why are they your friends?

21. Do you know if you have any enemies?

22. What do you think about drugs, alcohol, smoking and sex?

23. What's a fun thing that we could do together?

24. What qualities would you most want to see in a husband or wife?

25. Do you think prayer is important in your life?
26. What is the one thing that you would most like me to pray about for you?
27. Do you think you're an emotional person, and if so, why?
28. What do you think about your physical appearance?
29. Are you happy with your life right now?
30. How is your school life? Do you think your school is giving you the right support to progress in your education?
31. What do you think about your relationship with your siblings?
32. Do you think we treat you and your siblings fairly or differently?
33. What annoys you about [choose a subject] and why?
34. Are you a morning or night person?
35. Which adult do you like to talk to most and why?
36. Do you like to feel safe, or do you like adventure?
37. What makes you laugh?
38. Do you sometimes feel sad without knowing why?

39. Do you like our family, if not why?

40. What would your perfect day be like?

41. What career path would you like to pursue?

42. What holiday do you look forward to the most?

43. Are you studying as hard or as smart as you could be? Why or why not?

44. Would you like to own your company or have the security of working a 9 am - 5 pm job?

45. How do you unwind after a long day at school?

46. What are you looking forward to achieving?

47. Are you noticing any changes in your body?

48. Has anyone ever offered you tobacco, alcohol or drugs, and if yes what did you say?

49. What makes you happy or sad?

50. Are you having any feelings you can't explain?

51. Where would you most like to go on a family holiday?

NOTES/REFLECTION ON

51 Questions to Ask Your Child or Grandchild so You Know What to Pray For

ABOUT THE AUTHOR

Joy Ani is an ordained Pastor in Shalom Ministries International UK. She is the founder of 'Joy of Many Generations Ministries'—a ministry with a vision to Equip, Empower and Enable believers with disabilities so that they do not lose their joy, regardless of life's challenges.

Joy's passion is to see that children are well-nurtured, equipped and empowered through prayer so that they can withstand the challenges of life.

Joy is an author of the inspirational book '*Exchanging My Disability for God's Ability*', '*A Child's Guide to Prayer*', '*Activities and Colouring Prayer Book*', and other books. She shares her passion for writing through workshops for those who want to write their own books.

Joy has a BA (Hons) in Human Resources and Retail Management and holds a Diploma in Youth Counselling. She is married to Fidelis and they are blessed with three wonderful children and an amazing grandson.

OTHER BOOKS BY THE AUTHOR

Help My Heart

Exchanging My Disability for God's Ability

A Child's Guide to Prayer

Activities and Colouring Prayer Book

REFERENCES

Introductions
Ezekiel 22:30
Lamentations 2:19

CHAPTER 1
Children's Spiritual Well-Being

John 3:16
Luke 10:27
John 17:3
Psalm 42:1
Philippians 1:6
John 15:4-5
Hebrews 10:24
Ephesians 4:11-13
Psalm 9:10
Matthew 28:19-20
Genesis 4
Genesis 37-50
Ephesians 4:13

1 Peter 3:8

Ephesians 4:25-27

Isaiah 54:13

Jeremiah 29:11

John 16:13-14

Psalms 139:14

1 Corinthians 2:16

Colossians 3:23

1 Corinthians 6:18-20

Matthew 6:19-24

Proverbs 22:6

Deuteronomy 1:6

CHAPTER 2
Children's Physical Wellness

Luke 10:19

Romans 12:1

1 Corinthians 3:17

Romans 13:14

CHAPTER 3
Children's Interpersonal Relationships

Amos 3.3

2 Corinthians 6:14-15

Proverbs 13:20

1 Corinthians 5:11

Ezekiel 22:30

Lamentations 2:19

John 3:1

Luke 10:27

John 17:3

Psalm 42:1

Philippians 1:6

John 15:4-5

Hebrews 10:24

Ephesians 4:11-13

Psalm 9:10

Matthew 28:19-20

Genesis 4

Genesis 37-50

Ephesians 4:13

1 Peter 3:8

Ephesians 4:25-27

Proverbs 18:22

Isaiah 34:16

CHAPTER 4
Children's Educational and Career Progress

Isaiah 54:13

Jeremiah 29:11

John 16:13-14

Ps 139:14

1 Corinthians 2:16

Colossians 3:23

Psalms 90:17

Ecclesiastes.2:24

Colossians 3:23

Psalms 75:6-7

CHAPTER 5
Children's Financial Awareness

Matthew 6:19-24

Proverbs 22:6

Deuteronomy 1:6

Deuteronomy 8:18

Deuteronomy 28:12

CHAPTER 6
Children's Social and Emotional Mindfulness

Matthew 22:37

Philippians 4:6-7

Romans 12:2

Ephesians 4:26-27

Proverbs 25:28

Proverbs 17:22-23

1 Peter 5:7

Proverbs 4:23

https://www.thesun.co.uk/news/5963434/london-murder-rate-2018-city-highest-rate/

https://metro.co.uk/2019/09/25/many-deadly-stabbings-london-far-year-10804537/?ito=cbshare

Read more: https://metro.co.uk/2019/09/25/many-deadly-stabbings-london-far-year-10804537/?ito=cbshare

Dictionary definition: vocabulary.com

The free dictionary.com

Wealthwithpurpose.com

CHAPTER 7

Children — Scriptural Declarations

Ezekiel 22:30

John 17:3

Isaiah 54:13

Psalm 119:99

Luke 10:27

Psalm 42:1

Psalm 42:1

Jeremiah 29:11

Isaiah 54:13

Psalm 119:99

Psalm 139:14

Proverbs 15:13

Ecclesiastes 9:10

Proverbs 13:20

Proverbs 22:6

Proverbs 25:28

Psalm 90:17

Deuteronomy 15:6

Printed in Great Britain
by Amazon